T0151091

SAVINGS

POEMS BY LINDA HOGAN

COFFEE HOUSE PRESS :: MINNEAPOLIS :: 1988

Cover art by Nora Koch.
Back cover photograph by Richard Powers.

The author thanks the editors of the following publications in which some of these works first appeared: *American Voice, Bloomsbury Review, Blue Buildings, Crossing the River, Carriers of the Dream Wheel* (Harper & Row), *Chester Jones National Poetry Foundation 1986 Anthology, The North Dakota Quarterly, Prairie Schooner, Sing Heavenly Muse,* and *Tyuonyi.*

The author wishes to express gratitude to the Minnesota State Arts Board for generous support and assistance, to the National Endowment for the Arts, and to the University of Minnesota.

This project is supported in part by Elmer and Eleanor Andersen, The Jerome Foundation, The National Endowment for the Arts, a federal agency, and United Arts.

Coffee House Press books are available to the trade through our primary distributor, Consortium Book Sales and Distribution, 1045 Westgate Drive, Saint Paul, MN 55114. Our books are also available through all major library distributors and jobbers, and through most small press distributors, including Bookpeople, Inland, and Small Press Distribution. For personal orders, catalogs, or other information, write to:
Coffee House Press
27 North Fourth Street, Suite 400 Minneapolis, MN 55401.

Library of Congress Cataloging in Publication Data
Hogan, Linda.
Savings: poems/by Linda Hogan
p.cm.
ISBN 0-918273-41-2:
I. Title.
PS3558.034726S28 1988
811'.54—dc19   88-11819, CIP

10   9   8   7   6   5   4   3

Contents

Savings

Downstairs, things are growing.
Down stairs to the cellar
guinea eggs have quickened
and grapes have turned to wine.
Lye is burning through its tub
near potatoes with pale shoots,
and the molds are dividing
in jellies beneath wax,
that underworld
beneath the house with its bad family,
that world below
drumming
like old women
and blood stirring in the neck,
the older world
with its pale, thin roots of grass
and all things saved and growing.

Saving

My good clothes
hang in the back of the closet.
I've saved them
from shabbiness
the way my daughter puts an apple aside,
the way my mother saved her best towels
for the very last.

All these years the dandies have worn
their Sunday best
out on Friday,
slender hands and shoes too nice for wear
walking down the street
untied at day's end,
and don't all days end alike
with dark and rest
and children's prayers for life
rising up beyond the next
and next everything?

Night unravels
the calcium from bones.
Moths in the closet are growing
into dark holes they've eaten away
from fine shirts,
shirts empty of heartbeats,
all we should have lived for,
empty of arms that reach back
like a sleepless night, for what is saved,
all the way back
behind plaster
to the old world in canyons

with blood women dancing on walls
to the earth's drum
and the mother of deer and corn
so light the insects appear.

The invisible ones,
when we step this way
out of time,
are all around us.

In winter I remember
how the white snow
swallowed those who came before me.
They sing from the earth.
This is what happened to the voices.
They have gone underground.

I remember how the man named Fire
carried a gun. I saw him
burning.
His ancestors live in the woodstove
and cry at night and are broken.
This is what happens to fire.
It consumes itself.

In the coldest weather, I recall
that I am in every creature
and they are in me.
My bones feel their terrible ache
and want to fall open
in fields of vanished mice
and horseless hooves.

And I know how long it takes
to travel the sky,
for buffalo are still living
across the drifting face of the moon.

These nights the air is full of spirits.
They breathe on windows.
They are the ones that leave fingerprints
on glass when they point out
the things that happen,
the things we might forget.

Rooster,
the smaller he is,
the more he fills his chest with air
and crows.
He is not afraid of morning.
Nor is trout afraid, leaping into deadly air.
And I forget my own suspicions to follow some line
even with its hook:
Why don't you look me up sometime?

I'm going for the lure,
driving a highway,
wearing all my old lives,
scars on both knees
and crow's feet, a history
like broken fishline
carried by Old Whiskers
that Colorado fish, showing off
his escapes.

These are gods we follow,
sunlight or worm,
and we are trusting
as chickens walking to their death
along a hypnotic line of chalk
drawn by the good lord or Mesmer.

But the odds are good,
yes they are,
that sometimes we quit crowing
or chasing lunch. We forget running away
and stop in our tracks to listen

8   and hear the pull of our own voices
       like the Magi with their star,
       the wise ones with their camels,
       perfumes and gold,
       believing their inner songs,
       a journey in the bones of their feet,
       like migrating birds
       or salmon swimming ladders of stars
       to the beginning of life.

The New Apartment: Minneapolis

The floorboards creak.
The moon is on the wrong side of the building,

and burns remain
on the floor.

The house wants to fall down
the universe when earth turns.

It still holds the coughs of old men
and their canes tapping on the floor.

I think of Indian people here before me
and how last spring white merchants hung an elder

on a meathook and beat him
and he was one of The People.

I remember this war
and all the wars

and relocation like putting the moon in prison
with no food and that moon already a crescent,

but be warned, the moon grows full again
and the roofs of this town are all red

and we are looking through the walls of houses
at people suspended in air.

10   Some are baking, with flour on their hands,
or sleeping on floor three, or getting drunk.

I see the businessmen who hit their wives
and the men who are tender fathers.

There are women crying or making jokes.
Children are laughing under beds.

Girls in navy blue robes talk on the phone all night
and some Pawnee is singing 49s, drumming the table.

Inside the walls
world changes are planned, bosses overthrown.

If we had no coffee,
cigarettes, or liquor,

says the woman in room twelve,
they'd have a revolution on their hands.

Beyond walls are lakes and plains,
canyons and the universe;

the stars are the key
turning in the lock of night.

Turn the deadbolt and I am home.
I have walked dark earth,

opened a door to nights where there are no apartments,
just drumming and singing;

The Duck Song, The Snake Song,
The Drunk Song.

No one here remembers the city
or has ever lost the will to go on.

Hello aunt, hello brothers, hello trees
and deer walking quietly on the soft red earth.

First Light

In early morning
I forget I'm in this world
with crooked chiefs
who make federal deals.

In the first light
I remember who rewards me for living,
not bosses
but singing birds and blue sky.

I know I can bathe and stretch,
make jewelry and love
the witch and wise woman
living inside, needing to be silenced
and put at rest for work's long day.

In the first light
I offer cornmeal
and tobacco.
I say hello to those who came before me,
and to birds
under the eaves,
and budding plants.

I know the old ones are here.
And every morning I remember the song
about how buffalo left through a hole in the sky
and how the grandmothers look out from those holes
watching over us
from there and from there.

for Robin

What Has Happened to These Working Hands?

They opened the ground and closed it around seeds.
They added a pinch of tobacco.
They cleaned tired old bodies
    and bathed infants.
They got splinters from the dried-out handles of axes.
The right one suspected what the left was doing
    and the arms began to ache.
They clawed at each other when life hurt.
They pulled at my hair when I mourned.
They tangled my hair when I dreamed poems.
As fists they hit the bed
    when war spread again throughout the world.
They went crazy and broke glasses.
They regretted going to school where they became so soft
    their relatives mistook them for strangers.
They turned lamps off and on
    and tapped out songs on tables,
    made crosses over the heart.
They kneaded bread.
They covered my face when I cried,
    my mouth when I laughed.
"You've got troubles," said the left hand to the right,
    "Here, let me hold you."
These hands untwisted buried roots.
They drummed the old burial songs.
They heard there were men cruel enough to crush them.
They drummed the old buried songs.

It Must Be

I am an old woman
whose skin looks young
though I ache
and have heard the gravediggers call me
by name.

The pathologists come
with their forceps and gowns.
It must be a disease, they say,
it must be.

It must be, they say,
over there in the joints
that her grandmothers refuse to bend
one more time
though her face smiles at the administrators
taking reports.

The doctors come
with their white coats and masks.
It must be
her heart, let us cut her open with knives.

Doctor, did you hear the singing in my heart?
Or find the broken-off love, the lost brother?
Surely you witnessed all the old women
who live in the young house of this body
and how they are full of black wool
and clipped nails.

They make me carry on
under my jeans and sweater,
traditions and complaints about the sad
state of the nation.

They have big teeth
for biting through leather and birch bark
and lies
about the world.
They have garlic in their pockets
to protect us from the government.

The nurses arrive with pink nails
and the odor of smoke. They arrive
from lifting the hips of old men
as if they were not old men.

One of the old women inside
lashes out at the nurses
and all who remain girls,
and at bankers and scholars.
But despite that old woman,
there are days I see my girlish hands
and wonder which banker owns them
and there are nights I watch the wrong face
in the mirror, and afternoons
I hold that face down to the floor by its neck
with those banker's hands,
those scholar's hands
that wish to silence the old woman inside
who tells the truth
and how it must be.

And there are days
the old women gossip and sing,
offering gifts of red cloth and cornbread
to one another.
On those days I love the ancestors
in and around me,
the mothers of trees and deer

and harvests, and that crazy one
in her nightgown
baring herself to the world,
daring the psychiatrists to come
with their couches and theories and rats.
On those days the oldest one is there,
taking stock
in all her shining
and with open hands.

Life is burning
in everything, in red flowers
abandoned in an empty house,
the leaves nearly gone,
curtains and tenants gone,
but the flowers red and fiery
are there and singing,
let us out.

Even dying they have fire.
Imprisoned, they open,
so like our own lives blooming,
exploding, wanting out,
wanting love,
water,
wanting.

And you, with your weapons and badges
and your fear about what neighbors think
and working overtime
as if the boss will reward you,
you can't bloom that way
so open the door,
break the glass. There's fire
in those flowers. Set off the alarm.
What's a simple crime of property
when life, breath, and all
is at stake?

Morning with Broken Window

In the morning
and at night
wounded people stay close,
shoulder to shoulder
as if scar tissue will mend them together,
or the world's glue will stick them to life.
But sometimes I lift a cup of tea
and the handle falls off,
and continents crack in two
or someone sings a note that breaks the glass,
and they were just singing so who's to blame?

The whole world has been lying through its teeth.
People in bars will never love one another.
There's life within us.
Time to stop mowing its lawn
and severing the heads off its dandelions.

They're going to impound your car.
If that's all it takes to disillusion you,
just imagine the broken lives and wars of others.
So rip your gray dress at the seams,
tear things apart.
Frisk the ruins
and let the wicks of candles
burning inside you
shine a light in dark corners.
Hurry up now,
hurry.

The streets we live by fall away.
Even the asphalt is tired
of this going and coming to work,
the chatter in cars,
and passengers crying on bad days.

Trucks with frail drivers
carry dangerous loads. Have care,
these holes are not just holes
but a million years of history
opening up, all our beautiful failures
and gains. The earth is breathing
through the streets.

Rain falls.
The lamps of earth switch on.
The potholes are full
of light and stars, the moon's many faces.

Mice drink there in the streets.
The skunks of night drift by.
They swallow the moon.
When morning comes,
workers pass this way again,
cars with lovely merchandise. Drivers,
take care, a hundred suns look out of earth
beneath circling tires.

Geodes

We open
and there is that shining inside,
that light in the broken ones,
light in the woman unraveling threads
from grief's torn black cloth.
There's roaring light in the woman
holding seashells in her hand,
the one with red lava in her groin,
the woman with wild rice she harvested,
holy women
reading the world like a snake skin,
these women of earth's core
with amber earrings
who laugh and cry
in their brown shoes,
fight back in their jean jackets,
the woman
hugging a rag basket,
closing its open mouth
so it won't tell the story
of all the rags
and crystals of light
growing in the dark
and all the life growing
in the broken heart of things.

for freedom

The Young Boys

It's springtime and young boys
ride by, the moving spokes
of their bicycles like nothing.

They turn
as water in a wheel
or earth
with invisible speed,
the gods of Mount Olympus
bent over handlebars.

Come watch the race.
Stand at the corner
and give the drivers water with lime.
Don't tell them their wheels
are ready to collapse
at the end of the track.
Don't say how the black market is a bobbin
unwinding veins from living bodies
to fill itself.

Don't tell the beautiful gods on their bikes
about our other lives
in swamps, with trembling earth
and islands of peat floating up
growing cypress overnight
and the mosses
and birds with boomerang wings,
the goddesses of inner earth
bent over the cauldron.

Fishing

Stones go nowhere
while the river rushes them
dark with rain.
Fish are pulled out of their lives
by red-armed women on the banks
of vertigo.

What is living
but to grow smaller,
undress another skin
or scale
away rough edges
the way rivers cut mountains
down to heart.

We already know the history of sand,
and how days pass.
We know water and air
trying to break the spirit of stone.
We know our teeth grinding down
to their pith.

We know flint
all the way down to fire.
Go nowhere, be the fire.
Wait here for a nibble, you fishwomen,
stand where light is pared to a spark.
Be dust
growing to life.

Missing

Last night the crickets were gone.
I barely missed them singing
with my worries about dinner
and getting to work.

This morning the larder was empty.
The potato cellar held only clumps of earth.

I've forgotten years of my life,
the past, old songs, and all that.
My best dishes have been broken.

At noon the streets disappear
between white picket fences
clenched like teeth
smiling in offices.

On the avenue are earrings of the missing,
and jackets
empty on the twilight ground,
even a cap or two
without their heads

but down on the corner
a dark blue mail drop
is full of bad news, debts, and birth.
All our sorrows and living,
five-dollar checks to nephews,
even a ransom note
locked up on the dark corner.
It holds more life than we do!

And night without crickets
is full of red leaves
falling like letters the trees wrote
in a tongue we used to speak.
Read them, pick one up,
then another
and read them
and pay heed.

Pillow

There are nights with feathers underhead
I put an ear down
and listen for the voice of god
to rise up from the ticking.

Longer nights, I hold the pillow in my arms
like a lost child dreamed to life.

These feathers know the death rattle
of birch trees in white winter.
They roosted there alive one summer.

Pillow, forgive us the bird's lost life.
I smell it still,
my face against the singed dark,
and forgive us our other trespasses,
the mice within our poisoned walls,
the infirm in our beds,
and refugees driven in snow like rabbits
chased by a circle of beaters.

In this narrowing life, let us come apart
and float off
light like feathers
carried altogether in air
and coursing dark rivers.

Even the mountains have broken open
with light
while businessmen lean forward
peering in.
Light is breaking forth

from stone.
It shines out
touching all the perfect creases
of their hats and greatcoats,
and even white teeth
and bootblack shoes.

Breaking

When the forest was seed,
it wanted sun, rain,
and earth to break open.

Crows live in the heart
of the forest. They want the trees
to go back to seed.

Crow's dark life
the color of night
is stored sun,
grain
full of summer.

It lives like we live
off those before us,
those living in clay
whose bones survive
like broken pots
of tribes
that were here before our tribes,
that were here before the Americans
from broken worlds.

It is the breaking
that keeps going on.
There is no escaping the breaking
morning,
the tear in night
like a hole in a Mimbres pot
or a shell
life crawled out of

looking for the next world.

Tonight chickens sleep.
Dishes crack like a country
with its politics.
Even the polling booths at the drugstore
are broken.
Barns collapse like a house of cards
with a deuce too many.

Tonight in farm houses
people sleep
beneath quilts
the mothers made
even with heartaches
and beneath them and their slatted beds
and floors with splintered wood,
the tribes
and songs of iron
are ringing earth, wake up.

In the dark field
yellow squash is growing,
bones are filling up the arms
with new life,
gourds are climbing fences.

We give thanks
to deer, otter,
the great fish
and birds that fly over
and are our bones and skin.
Even the yelping dog at our heels
is a hungry crow
picking bones wolf left behind.
And thanks to the corn and trees.
The earth
is a rich table
and a slaughterhouse
for humans as well.

But this is for the elk,
the red running one
like thunder over hills,
a saint with its holy hoof dance
an old woman whose night song
we try not to hear.

This song is for the elk
with its throat whistling
and antlers
above head and great hooves
rattling earth.

One spring night, elk
ran across me
while I slept on earth
and every hoof missed
my shaking bones.

That other time, I heard elk run
on earth's tight skin,
the time I was an enemy
from the other side of the forest.
Didn't I say the earth is a slaughterhouse
for humans as well?

Some nights in town's cold winter,
earth shakes.
People say it's a train full of danger
or the plane-broken barriers of sound,
but out there
behind the dark trunks of trees
the gone elk have pulled the hide of earth
tight and they are drumming
back the woodland,
tall grass and days we were equal
and strong.

I don't remember when
the girl of myself turned her back
and walked away, that girl
whose thin arms
once held this body
and refused to work too hard
or listen in school,
said the hell then
and turned,
that dark child,
that laugher and weeper
without shame, who turned
and skipped away.

And that other one
gone from me
and me
not even starting to knot
in vein or joint,
that curving girl
I loved to love with,
who danced away
the leather of red high heels
and thin legs, dancing like stopping
would mean the end of the world
and it does.

We go on
or we don't,
knowing about our inner women
and when they left us
like we were bad mothers or lovers
who wronged ourselves.

Some days it seems
one of them is watching, a shadow
at the edge of woods
with loose hair
clear down the back
and arms with dark moles
crossed before the dress I made
with my two red hands.

You there, girl, take my calloused hand.
I'm going to laugh and weep tonight,
quit all my jobs and I mean it this time,
do you believe me? I'm going to
put on those dancing shoes
and move till I can't stand
it anymore,
then touch myself clear down
to the sole of each sweet foot. That's all
the words I need,
not poems, not that talking mother
I was with milk and stories
peeking in at night,
but that lover of the moon
dancing outside when no one looks,
all right, then, even when they do,
and kissing each leaf of trees and squash,
and loving all the girls and women
I have always been.

The Truth of Matter

Such lovely voices, the angels
singing at night in the showers,
sitting among plants
talking about their pasts on earth.

They don't care
about the inside of daily things
the bones in an open palm
or feet that start tapping
to inner songs.

Angels have better things to think about
than houses sitting on the shabby planet
with night lights in dark halls,
or attics, filled
with records of war and birth.

Angels have no time
for horses in the barn
or the three white geese.
They are busy preening their own wings
or pecking at one another.

But the demons
come knocking right on the door
telling how angels have failed
to look at the inside of lies and history,
at ticks on horses in the barn,
at broken beams of houses.
They point out the cat's thin ribs
and sore teeth.

I am back and forth,
held in soft wings
then falling, then saved,
dancing through air
to earth made of bones,
to new green rising up,
descending,
like the bountiful rain
taken in by earth,
taken in by sky.

Rain

Rain's story
falls to earth.
It tells corn
and wheat such tales
they believe
and rise up thin air.

This falling water is Africa rising.
Unfold the maps.
In all towns rain has fallen
life surged up
and turned to bones again.

Rain passes on
stories of people.
Some are loved in deep green jungles.
Some are tortured in mesquite hills.
In this town a man
was given something sharp to swallow
and no water. Rain said,
drink me.

Here they tell us, do not sing,
do not speak the name of rain
with its revolutionary
brewing of life
in death's harvest time.
Forget what has happened
in the round world.

Rain is banished
for making life

and carrying songs
and secrets
over state lines.
So tell this
from behind bars,
and the living rooms of homes,
from underground
where springs are flowing.

Tell your children
and mothers
rain beats on roofs,
men are forced to swallow sharpness,
flour sacks are pilfered by the full.
Lord have mercy.
Rain is falling.
It wants to touch our hair and skin,
wants to touch us,
and everyone knows
the stories of rain
and where it came from,
that's why they go inside
and bolt the door
and turn buttons of machines
off and on
even though the grass is growing back again
and everything we swallow
is the rain
and birth waters
are breaking down
the sturdy legs of sky.

The cold north wind
carries knives of ice. She wants
to steal your breath
and make it her own.

The southern wind
has warm hands.
She touches the arms of men
and they take off their shirts.

When the two winds meet,
the gentle wind of the south
is swallowed up into that angry wind,
that fast wind
that grows larger.

There is a lake in the north
where the two winds meet.
Once a man stood on shore
fishing and dreaming
of walleyes and his uncle's stories.
He was thinking of love
and going home
when the winds arrived
and he was trapped
between them
and turned to ice.

I know that man,
standing,
still standing,

and I know those winds

and the world
between them.

for Connie Brandenburg

Put down the dust rag,
unplug that coffee,
forget those black beans for supper!
Woman, you are nearly threadbare
and your sister, the wolf,
has been packed in your skin too long.
She's beginning to show through.

Leave well enough alone; serve her
notice of eviction and get back
to the miracle of putting your feet in brown boots
and stretching everything,
dollars, time, black beans,
even the moth-eaten skin you wore as a child.

Don't cock your ear that way.
There are no north country songs here,
so pretend you don't hear them.
Sharpen your fingernails, you
are nearly worn out
and animals have lasting souls,
even those goats
out on the rusting Fords.
And their hearts are stronger than men's
so don't let that animal pacing your skin
begin her song.
Don't let her sing
of long nights
or fear
of the human surrounding her.

Offering

Today the golden koi
were asking nothing of sunlight
and upper air,
but children fed them.
How lovely the gold and open fins
and the mouths gulping air,
breaking one world through another.

The feeders look like saints
in their kindness,
women throwing crumbs
on earth's table, what a feast!
Everything's a soup kitchen, a bread line
for the sweet.

Life gives life
and it's no great cost
so eat, sing,
offer this life of earth
back to earth.

And for the people,
down on their luck?
Never mind, you say,
even the earth has a cold eye
and wants to swallow us whole.

I go to work
though there are those who were missing today
from their homes.
I ride the bus
and I do not think of children without food
or how my sisters are chained to prison beds.
Now I go to the University
and out for lunch
and listen to the higher-ups
tell me all they have read
about Indians
and how to analyze this poem.

I ride the bus home
and sit behind the driver.
We talk about the weather and not enough exercise.
I don't mention Victor Jara's mutilated hands
or men next door
in exile from life
or my own family's grief over the lost children.

When I get off the bus
I look back at the light in the windows
and the heads bent
and how the women are all alone
framed in the windows
and the men coming home.
Then I see them walking on the avenue,
the beautiful feet,
the perfect legs
even with their spider veins,
the broken knees

with pins in them,
the thighs with their cravings,
the pelvis
and small back with its soft down,
the shoulders
which bend forward and forward
and forward
to protect the heart from pain.

There are things we do not tell
when we tell about weather
and being fine.
Our other voices take sanctuary
while police with their shepherds
stand guard
at the borders of breath
lest our stories escape
this holy building
of ourselves.

How did we come to be
so unlike the chickens
clucking their hearts out
openly in the rain,
the horses just being horses
on the hillside,
and coyotes howling
their real life at the moon?

We don't tell our inner truth
and no one believes it anyway.
No wonder I am lying
in the sagging bed,
this body with the bad ankle
and fifteen scars showing,
and in the heart, my god,
the horrors of living.
And in my veins, dear mother,
the beauties of my joyous life,
the ribs and skull and being,
the eyes with real smiles

despite the sockets they live in
that know where they are going.

Outside, the other voices are speaking.
Pine needles sing with rain
and a night crawler,
with its five hearts
beats it
across the road.

In silence
the other voices speak
and they are mine
and they are not mine
and I hear them
and I don't,
and even police can't stop earth telling.

The face of daylight has been removed.
Stars go on forever
about their lives.
Thank heaven,
the light is off in day's house
and everything can be itself.
The boar fears hunger.
The crab shelters herself with armor,
and we remove our clothes
and lie down afraid
of our own true colors.
At last,
emptiness admits it wants to steal your breath
but didn't I know it all along,
hearing those stars chatting
with their brothers, the stones,
and telling the truth.
Such honest dreamers we are
at night,
such honest tongues we wag,
but what liars in the morning
with our faces back on,
even the sky,
and we are liars at breakfast
and crossing ourselves
and our fingers
behind our backs
at five o'clock
and after dinner
when the dark puts her first card
down on the table.

Gamble

Those men with dollars on the mind
are pushed around by Monday
and tricked by Crow,
tricked by the broken look of Crow's thin legs.
That hungry Crow.
But its wings, oh!
Oh! and its laughter
and theft of radishes
from those big men's fingers
like a hand game
where dark women
deceive white men, singing,
You're crazy,
bad luck,
those words sounding like love songs
until the men pay up
with big grins on their faces.
Those women, oh!
in blue shoes
arm in arm
with their laughter.
They have even bilked the moon;
that's why I love them so
and why tonight is rich and dark.

The poor hands, overworked and dry,
dressing the body like maids
who button the lady's silk shirt
and fan her with their palms.

The poor palms
with their geography of lines.
One is broken,
another tells us, short life.

It is just like the hands
to tell their stories without shame.
Even held down, the white knucklebones
assert themselves through the skin.

One body, like a jury
split against itself.
Give them fish soup,
a loaf of bread
to sustain them in the night
when they think of guilt and innocence
and look at their lives,
how they were loved too little
or too much
and the mothers, dear god,
the mothers
nagged them for cracking their knuckles,
now no one will ever get ahead in this world
or be safe from sad loves
or debtors prison. No tie clasp
or credit card for that one.
Even their Salukis and greyhounds
are too thin.
A wonder anyone survives
what with the sad loves
and inner voices like dictators
carrying on all night,
and the mothers, dear god,
those mothers.

The House

The house
pays no attention to razor blades
dropped in its walls,
a disease of the marrow,
or skeletons of mice left between beams.
Like grandmothers perched on brown chairs,
it watches.

Lonely house.
Every corner had nine lives
and they all slept in one bed,
cooped up
those long winters
with candles, broth, and prayers.
Mice once scratched in the walls.

Poor house,
a candle lit for the hospital,
its wayward brother up on the hill
where Sisters of Mercy
turn away those without cash
now that churches and sickhouses
have gone the way of banks
with eyes that bolt shut
and all their animal life
turned to ribs.

But that house is looking over the town.
It's a grandmother, watching
and telling on you and on you,
watching cracks grow in the sidewalk,
earth pecking her way out.

The Avalanche

Just last month
the avalanches like good women
were headed for a downfall. I saw one
throw back her head
and let go of the world.

No more free soup bones for that one.
No more faces of friends at the door
with doilies and lace,
with ivory charms
carved of the elephant's great collapse.

Once an avalanche makes up her mind
not to cling,
there's no more covering up the cliff face
and hiding the truth,
and in her breakdown
she knows everything
and knows what she knows
about the turning wheel of earth,
love, markets, and even the spring
coming soon with its wildflowers.

The hands of wind are busy
wringing and tapping. You'd think
she was nervous from trying to make ends meet,
that wind,
wrapping her hands around the necks of trees
and shaking them out,
knocking against windows and walls
until houses give in.

There are days her slow song
remembers the names of men
walking alone by the sea
where oysters are wide open
knocking on stones.

Wind leans
against those men
like they are sails,
and against women,
their skirts bellows
for the fire of ourselves.
What fine weather.
What fine, fine weather.

The History of Fire

My mother is a fire beneath stone.
My father, lava.

My grandmother is a match,
my sister straw.

Grandfather is kindling like trees of the world.
My brothers are gunpowder,

and I am smoke with gray hair,
ash with black fingers and palms.

I am wind for the fire.

My dear one is a jar of burned bones
I have saved.

This is where our living goes
and still we breathe,

and even the dry grass
with sun and lightning above it

has no choice but to grow
and then lie down

with no other end in sight.

Air is between these words,
fanning the flame.

It is peaceful to cut celery
while the woman upstairs sings.

But the woman downstairs is drunk.
She hits the dog while I cook soup
and think of how our lives break
like windows from a flying stone
or glasses broken on a face.

I think I'll call the landlord
to say she's disturbing the peace,
but I chop carrots.

She's down to the dregs by now
and I'm cutting potatoes.
I know tomorrow she'll be outside
on her knees with their girlhood scars,
planting red tulips and petting her dog
while meat cooks on the stove.

I slice onions and think about all the broken souls
wandering about in worn-down shoes
and aching joints.

The woman downstairs is drunk.
The woman upstairs is singing
beneath the blue roof,
and I am boiling greens,
tomorrow's stew,
and in the basement
there are only damp walls and rotten wood
surrounding heat and electric,
and further down, deep thoughts of the forest,
mushrooms, the black coal
with its inner light.

Bridge

In straw
the pig was squealing
before the great silence.
The old woman stepped away
with blood on her hands,
wearing black.

Forgive me,
I am a coward
when it comes to screams and silence
and death
which I know in my mind
is just a crossing over
into the records of life and nothing.

It is a crossing over
like a bridge, all our swine life
eating from death's trough,
infant, mother, to nothing
but wind howling through the struts.

It is a crossing over this bridge
and this one
lifts its arms and swings them open
like the world's great mouth
letting boats with rich cargo pass through.

Everything passes
outward and in.
The houseboats with women and children pass,
the river passes, the voices
rising from the planks,

the mothers and old lady death
pass by the sow with her squeals
and all the hands
waving off death,
waving at life,
at the guard on duty overhead,
waving with all their might,
for all it's worth.

The Great Laws and Light

Have faith,
the great laws are still working
though we have tried to break them.
Gravity has not let go.
Autumn arrives.
Sun moves north and south.

But for us, where did it all go
wrong? Judgment Day's electric wire
frays behind beds where we sleep.
Gas leaks from pipes.
No tomorrow for some of us
tonight and nothing to believe in,
not light above ground
not earth below.

We break laws in darkness,
but still
light gets in
between the bars of a jail,
between courthouse beams and columns,
and members of the jury
with their twelve tight necks.

This morning without a gas leak
I was alive
and sunlight was on the floor
like silk stockings and yellow slip.
It snuck up to my bed.
Open windows.
Open doors.

The sun is sleeping on my bed,
touching my arm.
Warmth touches what was always there
and in the great laws
everything always is.

Night Wind

Come in, I'll hold you
with abandon
like water in my hands.

Come here, wind, singing beneath the door.
Pay no attention to that crow
calling from the aspens
or the red-winged ants wanting to fly.
Fill up the house with stories.
Tell of jungles
and coasts, even parking lots
in cities. What did the women wear
when they held you
like money?

Forget I said money
and the politics behind it.
Don't tell me the holocaust is always in the air,
trying to steal your breath
and mine.
Or how you were an illegal alien
crossing the border
riddled with bullets.

Wind, the crow wants you to leave
and take him along.
He's telling you
in this country the houses have walls
that stand up to your voice
breaking in
with terrible stories.

The red ants are waiting.
I know, I know
you are like breath
behind all words, even mine.

Two of Hearts

I dream my fingers are knives
I open
like a deck of cards
and read sunlight on the blades.

Two of Hearts,
born to a world of weapons.
Even your bones are knives
like the hands your neighbors conceal
with their glint of finger blades
clattering against tin spoons.

You would think
these hands that save birds,
hands that feed dogs
and heal the broken leg of a crane,
you would think the hands that love,
the Two of Hearts,
were always gentle.

Every morning
they turn back the quilt.
They offer cornmeal to the sun.
They brush hair.
These hands are full of God.

But I never forget
to recite history,
to recall the entire world
and all the young men
who became sergeants
with terror

disguised in their soft, loving hands,
the hands that hold hands with death,
and I am their blood,
no matter what,
and I am not their blood,
no matter,
but, oh, this world,
this cut and cutting world.

Knife

This knife was used to sever the cord,
mother and child.
This knife cut sugar from the tree.
This golden one
cut salt and spice. The blue one
opens up the rain's sky.
The one with a name
cut a wrist,
cut a neck,
frightened a child.
But this, this is a glass knife.
It cuts bread and berries.
When an angry person picks it up
how it wants to be broken.
Look at the moon on the edge of it,
and how the snail crawls the blade
and is not hurt.
It does not want to cut even the wheat,
this knife is so gentle.
When an angry person picks it up
scar tissue is already there.
The hand that holds it is a wound
and the eyes of the trees watch,
the eyes of the birds watch,
the eyes in the sky watch,
the eyes in stone watch.
All things watch and are still.

Neighbors

In this country,
the police shoot targets shaped like themselves.
Sometimes the targets shoot back.
Saturday governors throw clay pigeons
into blue sky.

This is the truth, not just a poem.
On this street, two men have shot themselves,
one held his wife and children hostage
from life and bills.

It is a nice street,
that's what they say,
where houses have helping hands in windows,
where in daylight
the curtains are laundered
in tubs and hung on lines.

But when dark comes,
even stars are bullets
in the sky's black belt.

In this country, men have weapons
they use against themselves
and others. It is the dying
watching death. Light a candle.
This is a poem and not just the truth
and they are not shadows
but bone, marvelous bone
that wants to walk upright
and skin, beautiful skin
that holds life in,
and hearts with their own chambers
of living, hearts

that want nothing,
not paychecks
on nightstands, not guns in the drawer,
nothing
but to knock on walls of the body,
let me in,
let me travel veins to the eyes,
light a candle
with the arteries in nervous hands,
and let me look out
on the beating world.

The soldiers on bivouac
with perfect creases
bend down behind the stone virgin
and throw dice.
The statue of Mary says:
      I'm too old for this, having journeyed so far
      with my heart this way and my poor legs
      hardening with veins.
      To hell with the soldiers and thugs
      and cops standing guard,
      with religion and capitalism
      and shooting craps.
      Up with the corn!
      Viva la chocolate!
      God save the black beans!

There's wailing in the distance,
not insects rubbing their wings
but someone crying out,
oh no oh god hail Mary.
His wife is shaking him:
      Get up. It's raining.
      The virgin is weeping
      out in the field behind the stone fence.
      She's weeping out there
      behind wet stones and soldiers.
      The rain is working away at human labors.
      The wall is crumbling.
      The soldiers have lost their creases
      and spit shine.
      Rain is taking apart the world,
      even our homes, our faces, our backs

with their tight muscles.
No more Great Wall of China.
No more Pietà.
Even Mary is being freed.
Get up. Get up.
There's a red lizard on Mary's shoulder.
Along the top of the hill
trees are growing out of stone,
trees that live with small nourishment,
and soldiers are singing
and the virgin is laughing.
Get up!

In the old days
she was a god
living in dark furrows
of earth-smelling earth,
that woman the stars were named for.

She was a god
living in the corn husk and silk
world that was torn open.

She was sister to the heat waves
rising up southern nights.
Don't come close!
Crony of red sky, she lived
beneath stones,
those progeny of stars
with their long waiting
for what?

Tonight she is exiled to cupboards and stoops.
Even the stars and moon
have fallen
over summer's edge,
burning like razed towns
charred heart and soul
to earth.

Surrounded by flames
she wants to sting herself
to death.
But sister,
we've all been surrounded

with no escape
from mean fire
and life or death,
and there's a whole continent
in this ring of fire,
breaking,
breaking into itself
with stinger and beak,
stopping its own watched heart,
that prehistoric heart
that remembers the gods
of furrow and corn.

That scorpion life
exiled to brown shoes and porches
knows something is wrong.

She is crawling
out the shoe,
that danger to bony feet.
Even the elements are at war.
I see,
I see
in the old days
we were all gods,
even the foot and its leather.
We were all gods
of shelter,
all this fiery life burning like wood,
and it does.

Those who thunder
have dark hair
and red throw rugs.
They burn paper in bathroom sinks.
Their voices refuse to suffer
and their silences know the way
straight to the heart;
it's bus route number eight.
They sing all day.
They drum
and at night
they put on their shawls and dance
thundering on wooden floors,
the feet saying
no more
no more
and those on floor number one
who are scrubbing
put down the gray cloth
and beat on the tiles. Take notice
we are done
with your scrubbing
and gluing together your broken stones
and with putting the open sign
around the neck of night
and bolting the sun to save your warehouse
from thieves and crooks.
You could say the sky is having a collapse,
you could say it's our thunder.
Explain to the president
why I am beating on the floor
and my name has been changed to

Those Who Thunder.
Tell him through the storm windows.
Those are fists he hears pounding.
Tell him we are returning
all the bad milk to the market.
Tell them all
we won't put up with hard words and low wages
one more day.
Those meek who were blessed
are nothing
but hungry, no meat or potatoes,
never salsa or any spice.
Those timid are sagging in the soul
and those poor who will inherit the earth
already work it
so take shelter,
take shelter you,
because we are thundering and beating on floors
and this is how walls have fallen in other cities.

In daylight
houses expand
like chests of majors.

In the dark night
they contract.
Don't be afraid,
it is only the house
breathing out
its daily war
with termites and slugs.

When walls and floorboards creak
we're afraid
of what gets in, light
from the next house
lying prone on the floor,
ten o'clock news,
a cat, wild
from the woods
and full of seed
stealing in the cracked door.
Even a child
from one night of love.
No place is safe from invasion
and everything wants to live,
even the moth
with eyes on its wings
flying in on light.

And upstairs, the bats are listening
with all their dark life

74

to what we can't hear,
to life and matter
in the eaves.
In true dark
the sound of wind arrives
all the way from stars
and dust from solar storms,
all the life wanting in,
even the moon at the window.